PRAISE FOR CLAY IN THE POTTER'S HANDS

"I thoroughly enjoyed *Clay in the Potter's Hands*. Diana Glyer's descriptions bring the process of creating pottery alive for us. She connects us to the men and women of Bible times for whom watching the potter at work would have been a daily experience. In so doing, she illustrates God's character and our discipleship in a unique and encouraging way. I recommend this book enthusiastically."

— CYNTHIA NICHOLSON

National Women's Task Force Coordinator, Vineyard USA, Assistant Pastor, Vineyard Church of Evanston, Illinois

"Most Christians have heard that God is the potter and we are the clay, but Diana Glyer, who has spent countless hours at the potter's wheel with her own hands saturated with clay, shows in this remarkable book that this saying is far more than a casual metaphor. God's fingerprints are all over us. As God hovers over his creation, centering us or shaping us or even restoring us from collapse, he may transform us in ways we never imagined. *Clay in the Potter's Hands* does a masterful job of revealing spiritual insights from an insider's perspective, as one potter considers the work of God the Master Artist. You will be challenged and inspired."

— JOSEPH BENTZ

Author of *A Son Comes Home, When God Takes Too Long,* and *12 New Testament Passages That Changed the World,* LaVerne, California

"In her book, Diana Glyer provides vivid and captivating imagery that brings delight in being mere clay in the hands of our mighty Creator. Inspiring questions accompany each chapter, culminating in prayers that lead the reader to a humble awe and gratitude for being chosen and crafted into the image of God by the Potter's own hand."

— DOUG GREENMAN

Executive Pastor, Stanwood Foursquare Church, Stanwood, Washington

"Before reading this book, I looked at the metaphor of the potter and the clay merely as a lesson of accepting the way God made me. This book has helped me see through the eyes of the potter and opened up a great many other lessons for me to meditate on. I felt so inspired by the lessons in the book."

— DANIEL COTHRAN

Missionary, Author of *Knowing the Difference: How to Recognize a Cult,* Tunghai University, Taiwan

"This is a book to be savored. Devotional books like this one are rare; I don't remember the last time I read one which expresses the richness of Scripture with such simplicity, grace and practical application. My own "crack-pot" life experienced the shaping, restoring and encouraging hand of the Potter through reading this book. I highly recommend the experience."

— WILL VAUS

President of Will Vaus Ministries, Author of *Mere Theology* and *The Hidden Story of Narnia*, Pastor of Stowe Community Church, Stowe, Vermont

"I find the general run of devotional books worse than useless; *Clay in the Potter's Hands* is a wonderful exception. A gifted writer who has thought long and hard about the Christian life and who has lived the biblical metaphor around which this work centers, she manages to be clear without being cloying, deep without being difficult, and spiritual without being sappy. She gives us everything the people who like devotional books are looking for without subjecting us to any of the things people who hate them are fleeing. This is a great achievement indeed."

— DONALD T. WILLIAMS

Pastor and Missionary, The Evangelical Free Church of America, Author of *Mere Humanity* and *Credo: Meditations on the Nicene Creed*, Professor of English, Toccoa Falls College, Toccoa, Georgia

"I was very impressed with the imagery of the clay (me) going through the process of becoming something useful. I have given several books to friends of all ages. My pastor commented that his 11 year old daughter could read it to her 7 year old twin sisters as well as her 80+ year old grandmother. The book has traveled all over to friends and family. Thank you for writing it and allowing us to be part of your creativity."

— RUTH E. CARLSON

Parish Nurse, Good Shepherd Evangelical Lutheran Church, Claremont, California

"Never has the most careful Old Testament scholar explained Isaiah's image of the potter and the clay (Is. 45:9) better than Diana Glyer in *Clay in the Potter's Hands*. Never again will I look at a clay pot in the same ordinary way. Neither will you. Read it slowly, devotionally, one chapter a day. Think on each chapter, pray over it, and find yourself molded, changed, enlightened, and encouraged."

— JOEL HECK

Professor of Theology, Concordia University Texas and Author of *From Atheism to Christianity: The Story of C. S. Lewis*

"Diana Glyer teaches like Jesus. This poetic parable of the pots got to my head and to my heart."

— GREG ANDERSON

Graduate School Chaplain, Wheaton College, Wheaton, Illinois

"This is a really good book! It manages to combine depth and simplicity which is rare, but I think it is the way it treats our experience of pain and broken-ness which really sets it apart. The chapters on Returning, Repairing and Redeeming were especially moving and significant for me. This book is going to be so helpful to so many people!"

— MALCOLM GUITE

Priest, Poet, Chaplain at Girton College, University of Cambridge, Author of *Faith, Hope, and Poetry*, Cambridge, England

"*Clay in the Potter's Hands* is a strong, extended metaphor that takes what is already a good analogy and makes it much more profound. When we hear the Apostle Paul say that we are like clay to God the Potter, we hardly realize that each stage of the process of shaping the artisan's work serves as a unique analogue to something that God does in the process of shaping us. In our modern world of prefab housewares, that analogy could well have been lost, had not Glyer recaptured it for us."

— JAMES W. MILLER

Senior Pastor, Real Life LA, Author of *God Scent: A Devotional*

"I used Diana Glyer's *Clay in the Potter's Hands* for my Ceramics classes. The students loved identifying with well known Biblical stories as they worked at mastering the potter's wheel."

— SUSAN NEY

Artist and Professor, Azusa Pacific University, Azusa, California

"Rarely does one encounter a writer who seizes a powerful metaphor, digs deeply into its heart, and allows it to shape and inform not only her prose but her life. In *Clay in the Potter's Hands*, Diana Glyer has done just that. Here, we gently move from observer to participant and from casual knowledge to redeeming wisdom. Each step of this shaping process is filled with meaning and each meditative moment is touched with the eternal hand of the Master Potter. Diana Glyer invites her readers into the real potter's studio."

— SCOTT B. KEY

Professor of Philosophy, California Baptist University, Riverside, California

"Fascinating! As a potter, I could identify with the different stages of creating with clay, and as a Christian, I appreciated how this book ties each step into how God works in our lives. From the beginning to the end—God is able to use us—if we are yielded and still. Thank you for this insight and testimony of faith which has enriched my life."

— PAT BALLARD

Artist, Westchester, California

"I've read dozens of devotional books. Ok, well, I've started dozens of them, but with very few exceptions they usually leave me uninspired. But Diana Glyer has managed the nearly impossible: to sound the deep places of the heart with healing, humor, wisdom and grace. The way she does it—suggesting rather than saying, leaving all kinds of room for the reader—makes this book uniquely effective in all of the devotional reading I have ever done. I read one chapter a day, and without fail always felt the Great Physician using Diana's care-filled, honest humility and spare, rich prose to open up my heart for that divine surgery that cuts even as it cleanses. I do not exaggerate to say that I left tears of joy, release, refreshment and grace on every single page. It's that good. It's better—it's superb and so full of grace and truth that it has become a profound treasure. *Clay in the Potter's Hands* moved me to the depths of my soul."

— ANDREW LAZO

Speaker, Co-editor of *Mere Christians: Inspiring Stories of Encounters with C. S. Lewis*

"In one hundred pages, Diana Glyer offers her readers fifteen marvelous chapters for reflection and more. You can "feel" her love of pottery and join her as she tells the story of creating something beautiful. Each chapter of *Clay in the Potter's Hands* offers the reader an opportunity to accompany the potter at work. The author gently and easily moves from the potter's wheel to texts from the Bible that offer examples of each stage of development of the artist's work. These are accompanied by marvelous insights and questions for the reader to consider; then each chapter concludes with a prayer that brings the entire segment together quite nicely. As a Jesuit, I found this work very appealing. St. Ignatius suggested the use of imagination for contemplative prayer. The Scripture texts that Glyer has chosen, together with the fascinating story of making and repairing pottery, would alone be helpful toward contemplative prayer. However, she has gone further. Each chapter is a movement from the wheel where clay is worked to a "wheel" where a healthy spiritual life is formed. The entire book could be read rather quickly, but I suggest that the reader savor each chapter as a daily prayer. There will be no disappointments."

— FATHER JOHN CHANDLER

Honolulu, Hawaii

Clay in the Potter's Hands

Leader's Guide

Second Edition

Clay in the POTTER'S HANDS

Leader's Guide
Second Edition

Bethany Wagner
BASED ON THE BOOK BY
Diana Pavlac Glyer

Photography by Adam Bradley
Design by Matthew K. Tyler

Lindale & Assoc.
A Division of TreeHouseStudios

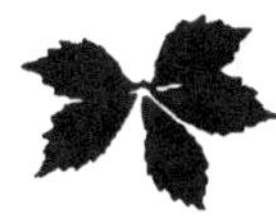

THIS LEADER'S GUIDE IS SPECIFICALLY DESIGNED TO BE USED WITH CLAY IN THE POTTER'S HANDS BY DIANA PAVLAC GLYER, AVAILABLE IN PAPERBACK AND ALSO AS AN EBOOK AT AMAZON.COM. FOR MORE INFORMATION ABOUT THIS AND OTHER CLAY IN THE POTTER'S HANDS RESOURCES, PLEASE VISIT WWW.DIANAGLYER.COM.

CLAY IN THE POTTER'S HANDS LEADER'S GUIDE: SECOND EDITION

BETHANY WAGNER AND DIANA PAVLAC GLYER

COVER PHOTO AND DESIGN BY MATTHEW K. TYLER.
INTERIOR DESIGN BY MATTHEW K. TYLER.
INTERIOR IMAGES BY ADAM BRADLEY AND MATTHEW K. TYLER.

ISBN-13: 978-1-937283-15-5

1. SPIRITUAL FORMATION. 2. CHRISTIAN LIFE.

SECOND EDITION 9 2020

To Glen and Kathleen Wagner, my first and favorite teachers, and to all my fellow travelers on this beautiful, daunting, wondrous journey Christ is shaping day by day.

CONTENTS

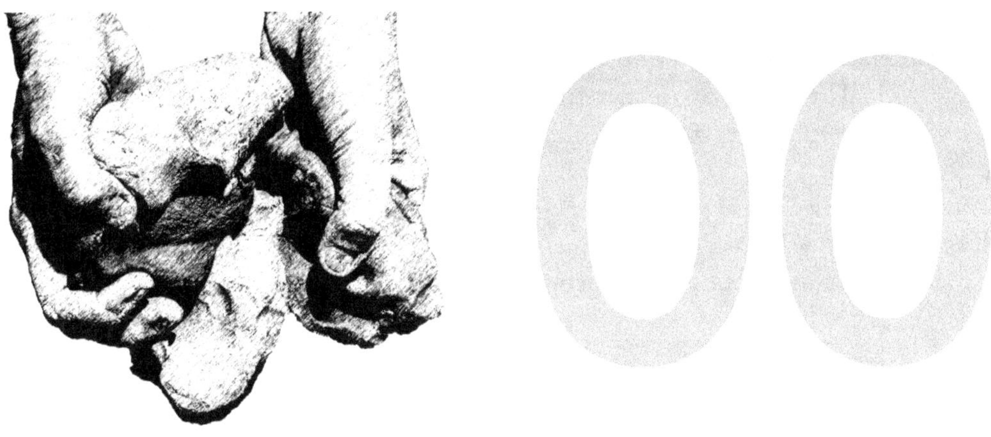

INTRODUCTION

So you have decided to lead a small group study. Congratulations! This is a challenging task, sometimes daunting, but also a richly rewarding one that can transform your own life. There is nothing quite like seeking the Lord in community. Here are some suggestions to consider as you embark on this journey.

ABOUT CLAY IN THE POTTER'S HANDS

Isaiah 64:8 reads, "Yet you, LORD, are our Father. We are the clay, you are the potter; we are all the work of your hand." Throughout Scripture, God is referred to time and time again as a potter. And we are his clay.

This book shows that this is far more than a casual metaphor. As God hovers over his creation, centering us or shaping us or even restoring us from collapse, he may transform us in ways we never imagined. The author guides the reader chapter-by-chapter through the process of creating pottery and illustrates the powerful spiritual truths behind each step.

Clay in the Potter's Hands has been used in home groups, Bible studies, Sunday school classes, Lenten devotions, one-on-one discipleship, and other group settings in churches, homes, and schools. The book itself contains discussion questions and a prayer at the end of each chapter, but this workbook helps groups interact more closely with the text, providing prompts and space for participants to record their own notes, ideas, questions, observations, and prayers.

ABOUT THE WORKBOOK AND LEADER'S GUIDE

As you will discover throughout this study, God shapes people with care and works in miraculous ways in every life. But this does not mean that every person's spiritual journey will look the same; in fact, like handcrafted pieces of pottery, each is entirely unique.

That's where the workbook comes in, helping participants discover how their stories fit into the narrative of the pottery process and what the image of God as a potter means in their individual lives. And as a leader, this guide will equip you with further key points, questions, and "next steps" designed to foster discussion, deeper understanding, accountability, and growth.

When studying *Clay in the Potter's Hands*, it is ideal to have time for individual study as well as group study. If your group consists of more than 10 people, some time for discussion and prayer in smaller groups of 3–4 people would also be helpful.

FORMATTING YOUR STUDY

The most straightforward way to complete *Clay in the Potter's Hands* is to meet for weekly sessions, completing one chapter a week for 15 weeks. Allowing 1-1 1/2 hours per session is suggested.

That being said, this study is well suited to fit a variety of group sizes and time frames. Depending on the needs of your unique group, you may spend more time on one chapter in particular, or combine two or three chapters during one week. If you are doing a Lenten study, completing 2 chapters each week would fit your timeline well.

But whichever time frame you choose, I suggest having all participants read the chapter, take notes in the workbook, and complete the respective workbook questions and prompts before you meet. Then during your group sessions, you can dive right away into discussing the chapter and your experiences with the text, as well as spending significant time in prayer.

THE 5-SESSION STUDY

Clay in the Potter's Hands also fits well into a 5-session study, as outlined below:

SESSION ONE: INTRODUCTION

This first chapter, "Creating," is the basis for the rest of the book, discussing the nature of God as creator and humanity as his creation. It establishes some key principles that apply to the rest of the book before chapter 2 starts in on the step-by-step process of creating a piece of pottery. In your first session, go through chapter one and discuss how your group wants to learn and grow over the course of your study.

SESSION TWO: PREPARATION

Chapters 2–6 focus on the preparation steps of pottery as the potter finds the clay and prepares it to be shaped on the wheel. These are the necessary steps all pottery must go through before its true shape comes into formation.

SESSION THREE: FORMATION

Chapters 7–11 cover the critical formation steps as the potter guides the clay into its final shape as a pot, cup, bowl, or vase.

SESSION FOUR: COMPLETION

Chapters 12–14 contain the final steps after the clay has been shaped as the potter repairs any damage, re-fires the pottery, and even redeems any shattered pieces.

SESSION FIVE: CONCLUSION

In your last session, wrap up your study with the final chapter, "Abiding." This chapter concludes the long process you have started, and helps participants identify where they are in the pottery process, as well as what next steps they should take as creations of God. Finish with a group prayer for the future work of God in each person's life.

THE WEEKEND STUDY

The 5-week format is also ideal for a weekend retreat or 2–3 day church event. For these more intensive studies, be sure to set aside time for solo study, small group discussion, and instruction as a whole group. I suggest the following structure for a weekend study:

1. Begin each session by introducing the chapter(s) to the entire group. Talk through the potter's steps and the specific actions the potter takes, before moving on to how this illustrates God's creative work forming and shaping us.

2. Break apart for solo time, so each participant can read the material alone, take notes, and answer the workbook questions.

3. Join together again in small groups of 3–4 people to discuss the material, share answers to questions, go through each of the Scriptures in the workbook, and prayer for one another.

4. Come together as a whole group to share any observations as a whole and begin the next session.

THE LENTEN STUDY

Here are some thoughts to consider as you lead a study during Lent. This book takes you through a process, anticipating and arriving at the final step: completion of the pot and sanctification of the person. This echoes the process of Lent, as we dwell on our own humanity and brokenness, and wait with eager anticipation the resurrection of our Lord—"the goal of your faith, the salvation of your souls" (1 Peter 1:9). It may be helpful to keep this parallel in mind throughout your study.

SOME FINAL SUGGESTIONS

— Whatever time frame you choose, begin and finish each session with prayer, praising God for his work as Creator and asking him to direct your study.

— Encourage and hold each other accountable to complete the reading and workbook material for each session, and to be honest and authentic with one another as you encounter ways God is shaping and directing you.

— The chapters are short enough that you can read them aloud together. You might read the chapter and then discuss it, or read the next week's reading at the end of each session. Or take turns reading aloud, paragraph by paragraph around the circle.

— You will find additional resources at www.DianaGlyer.com. And we would love to get your feedback on how we can improve the book and workbook, answer questions, or offer additional resources.

— Finally, pray regularly for the individuals and spiritual growth of your group. And know that we are praying for you.

May the Lord richly bless you as you begin this journey together!

Bethany Wagner
Portland, Oregon

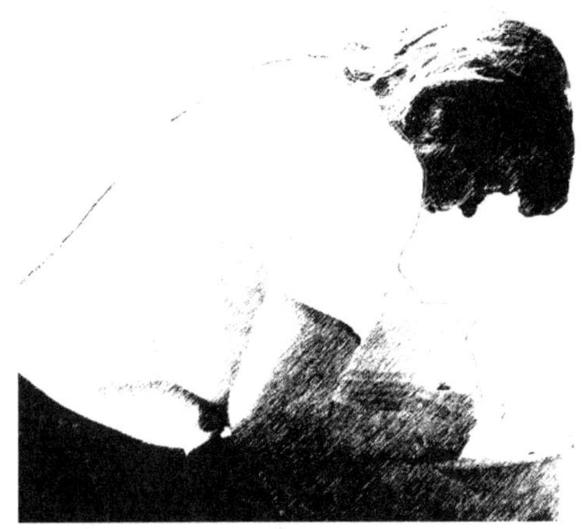

CREATING

"Throughout the Bible, God uses word pictures to tell us what he is like. God is like a loving shepherd. A good neighbor. A strong tower. Of all the pictures that God offers, one of the earliest and most persistent is this: God is like a potter, and we are like clay."

INTRODUCTION

This first chapter is the basis for the rest of the book, establishing some key principles before Chapter 2 starts in on the step-by-step process of creating a piece of pottery.

At its heart, this chapter asks a simple but deep question: what does it mean to create? Specifically, what does it mean that God created and continues to shape us? According to Genesis, God creates the universe on a rushed, large scale. But then he creates man—the most significant part of his creation—on a hushed, small, intimate scale.

DISCUSSION

GOD DRAWS NEAR

"The potter must stoop low over the pot to shape it; pottery making depicts a creator who stoops low and draws very near."

The potter stoops low over the pot and draws near. In the same way, Jesus came down, touched lepers, hugged sinners, and shapes our lives today. Share a time in your life when you felt closest to God, and felt his hand working in your life.

GOD IS INTIMATELY INVOLVED

"Clay gets all over the potter as the potter works with the clay; pottery making illustrates God's constancy and intimacy."

Clay gets all over the potter as he works with the clay. In the same way, God intentionally entwined himself with history and humanity through Creation, the Incarnation, and the giving of the Holy Spirit. How is God involved in your life? How are your choices and everyday life different because of your relationship with him?

GOD MARKS US AS HIS OWN

"Clay responds sensitively and permanently to the touch of the potter; pottery making represents God's certain touch on our lives."

The potter leaves fingerprints all over the moist, malleable clay. In the same way, our lives are a testament to our Creator, who shapes us daily. In what ways do Christians bear Christ's mark? How do—or should—others recognize God's people?

List several times you have clearly seen the fingerprints of God in the circumstances of your life. Then take time to thank God for it!

KEY QUOTE

"The Lord God formed the man. And look at how he did it. The word that is translated 'formed' comes from the Hebrew word yatsar, and yatsar refers to forming, stretching, squeezing, pressing, and molding something into a specific shape."

KEY SCRIPTURES

Have members of the group take turns looking up and reading these passages:

Jeremiah 18:1-6
Isaiah 29:16
Isaiah 45:9
Isaiah 64:8
Romans 9:21
2 Corinthians 4:7
2 Timothy 2:20-21

NEXT STEPS

It's time to put what you have studied and discussed into practice. Have members of the group take on one or both of these "next steps" and come back next week to share the results before beginning the next chapter.

1. Make a point to create something this week, whether a painting, a poem, a story, a coloring page, a doodle, a meal, etc. Think about the process. What do you invest of yourself in your creation? What does your creation say about you and your experiences?

2. Contemplate how God may be molding and transforming you right now, in this season of your life. Over the course of this week, pray for one another's transformation by God daily, and for the group as a whole. You have an exciting journey ahead of you!

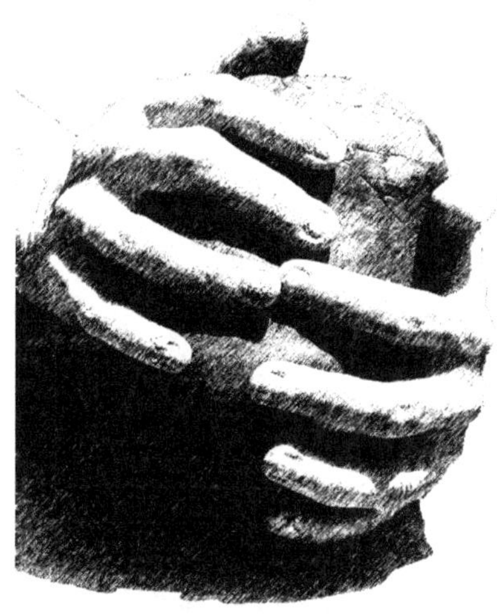

SEARCHING

The potter walks along the creek bank, and then climbs the narrow path into the surrounding hills. He is searching for clay. It is buried along riverbanks, hidden by dense undergrowth. The potter hikes far from home, climbs into the hills, searches through forgotten pathways. Deep into the wilderness. As a miner looking for jewels. As a shepherd searching for his lost sheep. As a loving God calling for his children.

INTRODUCTION

Surrendering ourselves to be shaped by God is hard, painful, and sometimes scary. We give up comforts. We give up control. We come, imperfect, to serve a perfect God.

A perfect God, yes. But also a God who loves us wildly, who searches for us and knows us more deeply than we know ourselves. This chapter establishes this all-important message of hope.

In the weeks to come, we will come face-to-face with the challenges and trials of life, as well as our own shortcomings. So in this session, be sure to emphasize that throughout this, God loves us and is constantly seeking to draw us back to him. And because of this, we can trust him with the challenges ahead. We can trust the Potter's hands with our future.

Depending on the scope of your group, there may be members who have never encountered the love of God before. In asking the first question, be sensitive to the responses given, and be prepared for individual follow-ups if needed. Be sure they know that you and any other leaders are available if they want to know more about following Christ.

DISCUSSION QUESTIONS

GOD SEARCHES FOR YOU

"God loves us, values us, eagerly seeks for us, and rejoices over us when we are found."

God has been seeking you all of your life. If you have responded to his call, take time now to thank him for the way he has made you his own. If you have never responded, take time now to consider what it might mean for you, a wandering lamb, to be found and taken home to his fold. Then find someone who can tell you more about the Good Shepherd who loves you.

GOD IDENTIFIES YOUR UNIQUE TRAITS AND HANDLES YOU ACCORDINGLY

"A good potter recognized the unique and beautiful qualities of each type of clay. The amount of pressure that the clay can tolerate, the amount of heat that it needs to reach its potential—these factors and more will vary from clay to clay, and the good potter understands the differences."

Each type of clay has unique qualities; each of us is unique in personality, abilities, and gifts. God desires to meet you where you are and calls you to use your traits and gifts as his unique creation. Share some ways in which you are a unique lump of clay. Have everyone in the group fill in the blank: "I am ______________________________." What makes you unique? What personality traits, quirks, and gifts do you have? And what might your answers say about how God is shaping you?

KEY QUOTE

"Wise potters know how to adapt to the particular temperament of the clay. And God in all his wisdom knows what is best. He has searched me and known me and called me by name."

KEY SCRIPTURES

Have members of the group take turns looking up and reading these passages. What does each story say about God and His love?

PARABLE OF THE LOST SHEEP: Luke 15:1-7
PARABLE OF THE LOST COIN: Luke 15:8-10
PARABLE OF THE PRODIGAL SON: Luke 15:11-32

NEXT STEPS

As seen, the focus of this chapter is on the acts of God as he searches for us, like a potter for clay, and knows us inside and out. This week, ask God to show you how your unique qualities are strengths that he can use, and set aside some time to listen sensitively to how he is shaping you.

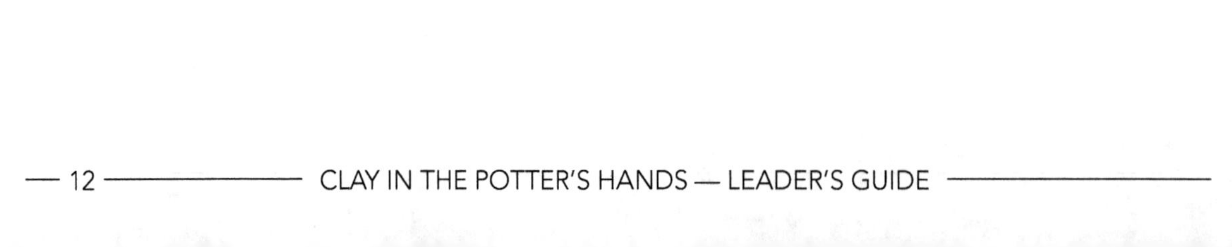

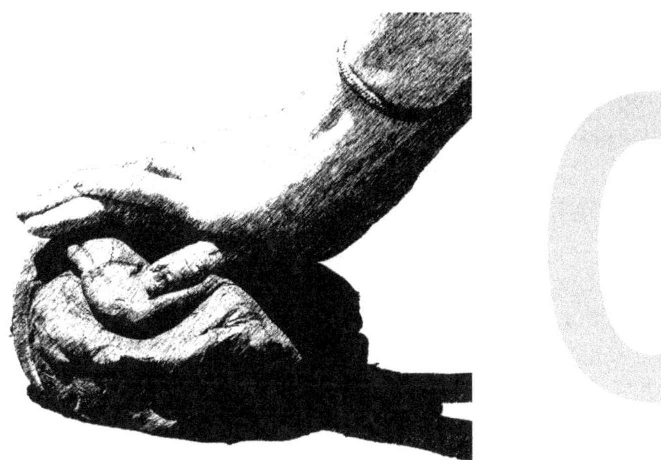

03

PREPARING

"By the time the potter finds the clay and digs it out of the ground, it has been pressed into the earth for quite a while. As a result, certain impurities are embedded in it. There are small rocks, twigs, and bits of leaf and bone, all the result of having been pressed against the world…The clay looks great: clean and smooth and pure. But if these foreign objects are not removed, there will be very serious consequences later in the process."

INTRODUCTION

These next two weeks focusing on "Preparing" and "Committing" are about support, encouragement, and accountability. As a group, you will identify things present in your lives that distract and damage, and rest together in God's faithfulness to cleanse us from all unrighteousness. Then we can move forward into becoming the people he created us to be.

DISCUSSION QUESTIONS

IDENTIFY SINS AND DISTRACTIONS

"The clay looks great: clean and smooth and pure. But if these foreign objects are not removed, there will be very serious consequences later in the process."

The book includes the question, "Are there things in your life, large or small, that God wants to remove from your life because they hurt his heart and injure other people?" Take some time to confess to one another.

Is there anything in your life that, while perhaps good on its own, has turned into an idol distracting you from becoming all God wants you to be? Some examples could be social media, television, busyness, work, or certain relationships. Take some time to share and confess to one another and the Lord.

Are there people you need to talk to in order to settle a matter that has caused stress, tension, shame, or uneasiness? (Sometimes it's best not to say their name out loud!) Ask for God's wisdom and grace in the situation.

GOD IS FAITHFUL TO CLEANSE

"Because this is such a serious matter, the wise potter takes extra care at this stage of the process. The clay is cleaned of every kind of impurity. It is carefully examined, and stones, sticks, and other materials are carefully removed. It might even be put through a screen in order to eliminate even the smallest thing that might be harmful."

Answering the above questions is hard, especially in the presence of others. But once we have identified problem areas in our lives and laid them all out on the table, we are stronger than ever, and stand ready for God to shape us and "lead us in the way everlasting" (Psalm 139:24).

Pray through Psalm 51 out loud, placing yourselves in God's hands and asking him to redeem and cleanse.

KEY QUOTE

"A little sliver of wood, a tiny stone, a seed, root, or twig. It is possible that such things will stay hidden for a long, long time. But in the firing process, in the heat of the kiln, nothing can stay hidden for long."

KEY SCRIPTURES

Have members of the group take turns looking up and reading these passages:

Psalm 103:8-12
Psalm 139:23-24
Micah 7:18-20
Hebrews 4:12-13
Hebrews 12:1-12
1 John 1:9

NEXT STEPS

We've answered the hard questions. Now, this week, take concrete steps to identify and remove or repair things in your life distracting or causing damage to you, your relationship with God, or others. Encourage the group members to support each other and hold one another accountable in love.

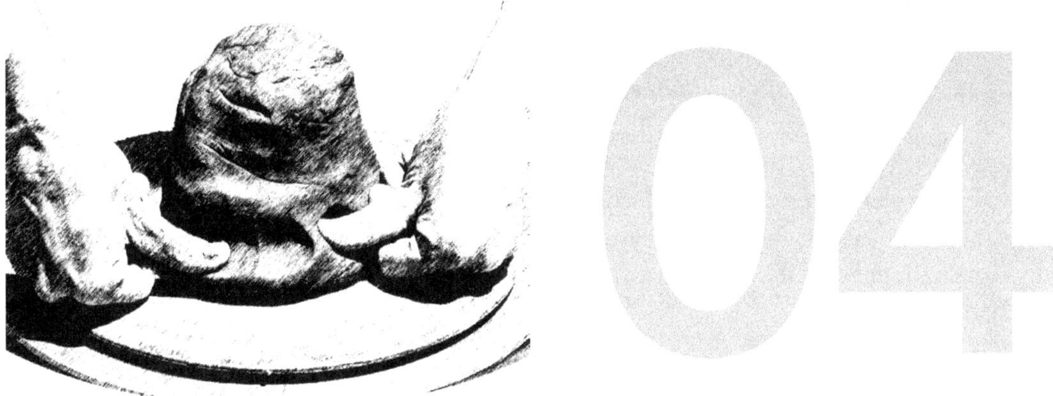

COMMITTING

After the clay is completely cleaned, it is wedged, a process that looks a lot like kneading dough. It is an important step, requiring patient attention from the potter. It involves a satisfying rhythm of pressing, turning, pressing, turning.

INTRODUCTION

Commitment is about harmony, accord, and being of one mind, and this is the kind of solid relationship God wants to have with each of us. This chapter, a crucial step in the process of crafting a pot, has two important steps applicable to our lives. First, we have that moment of commitment when we first decide to devote our lives to Christ. But second, and perhaps even more important, is the step of keeping that commitment and harmony. This is the challenge, and this is the battle worth fighting.

DISCUSSION QUESTIONS

MOMENTS OF COMMITMENT

"Moments of commitment are all around us: they are clear, measurable, memorable, powerful."

As a group, share some moments of commitment you have gone through. What was easy about the commitment? What was hard and maybe scary? Have you ever doubted that commitment?

What was your moment of commitment to Christ like?

Has God convicted you of any area of your life that is not going well because you haven't made a decisive commitment? If so, take time to make that commitment sure.

REMAINING COMMITTED

"We commit our lives to Christ. And having made that commitment, we persevere. We resist the temptation to give up. We stick with it, even when it becomes inconvenient, annoying, uncomfortable, or dangerous to do so."

As you have probably experienced, what makes commitment hard is usually not the initial moment of committing, but the daily choice to remain committed through the everyday tasks and challenges of life. What in your life tempts you away from complete commitment to Christ?

Together, brainstorm some ways we remain committed to our jobs, our families, our goals and dreams, our spouses, and our God during the daily grind of everyday life.

KEY QUOTES

"I like to think of it as clay brought into harmony, all parts of it balanced and at peace. In James 1:7, it says that when we are double-minded, we are unstable in all our ways. With great care and patience, the potter wedges the clay so that all of the clay particles are in accord, and so that every part of that clean ball of clay is stable and strong."

"Following God means cultivating faithfulness. He tells us we shouldn't put our hands to the plow and then look back—the work gets done when there is commitment and single-minded, persistent devotion."

KEY SCRIPTURES

Have members of the group take turns looking up and reading these passages:

Psalm 37:3-6
Proverbs 16:3
Luke 9:57-62
Philippians 3:12-14
2 Timothy 4:6-8

NEXT STEPS

Think about the long-term projects that you are in the midst of. List them. Then ask for God's help in strengthening your resolve and finishing well.

Finally, pray through Psalm 119:57-64 together. Commit together to seek after the Lord, and encourage one another and hold each other accountable.

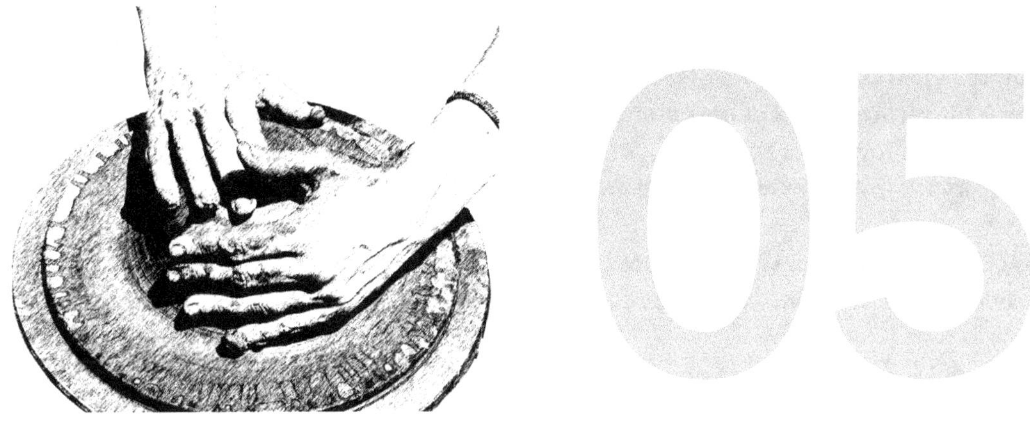

CENTERING

Before the clay can be formed into a pot, it must be centered, so that every part of it lines up with the very heart of the wheel. The unruly clay wobbles at first, heading off in all directions. The potter adds water and presses his hands against the sides of the clay as it spins, pushing the clay closer to the wheel head, smoothing uneven places, and pressing bumpy edges. Finally, under the firm and gentle guidance of the potter, the clay begins to center. It is a process that requires much time, trust, and patience. But by the end, the clay will be smooth, solid, and perfectly aligned—on its way to becoming a true work of art.

INTRODUCTION

Remember that harmony we talked about in the last chapter? For clay, that harmony is reached through the process of centering, perfectly aligning with the wheel. For us, that harmony and peace is reaching by aligning ourselves with the heart of God.

This chapter, then, could also be titled "Integrity." Christ sought you, and you responded with surrendering and commitment. Now, what does it look like if you bring the entirety of your life—work, school, home life, relationships, leisure, actions, thoughts, word—into alignment with your commitment to Christ? It isn't easy, but the result is peace.

DISCUSSION QUESTIONS

CENTERING IS A PROCESS

"It may take a surprisingly long time.... I know that clay can't speak, but I've often thought that if it could, it would definitely express impatience at this point in the process."

Reflect on your schedules this past week. Was it characterized by joy and peace, ease and strength? Or was it marred by fearful striving? Were you able to find moments of Shalom despite the push and pull of life's circumstances?

Brainstorm together practical ways to facilitate this concept of centeredness and aligning your everyday life with God's good plan for you.

CENTERING INVOLVES WAITING ON GOD

"Shalom is the peaceful fruit of God's initiative, God's labor, God's faithfulness, and not my own."

Although we can take steps to invite centeredness and Shalom into our lives, it is ultimately a work of God. What are you waiting on the Lord for? Pray for patience together as God works sometimes slowly, but always surely, to bring about centered peace in your life.

PEACE THROUGH CENTERING

"[Shalom] means doing things with natural ease, not with frantic force or fearful striving. It means responding to life's challenges with a sense of creativity and optimism and resilience. It is a sense in my body and soul of well-being, safety, harmony, vibrant health. To be at ease, inside and out. Shalom. Aligned."

Take time to read, meditate on, and discuss the above quote together. Have group members envision their lives infused with this Shalom, every area and decision completely aligned with God. This is how we become the best versions of ourselves; by complete centeredness with our Creator.

KEY QUOTE

"That wobbly, bumpy, misshapen lump of clay rests under the skill of the potter's hands, and as a result it becomes smooth, solid, and centered. And so it is with my soul."

KEY SCRIPTURES

Have members of the group take turns looking up and reading these passages:

Isaiah 40:28-31
Philippians 1:3-6
Philippians 4:4-7

NEXT STEPS

Time to get specific: What changes do you need to make in your life so that the Great Shalom, the peace of God, is an ever-increasing part of your daily life? Focus on making those changes this week. It may mean setting aside time each day to realign yourself with God's peace. It may also mean revising the way you speak, work, or think to incorporate God into every facet of your life.

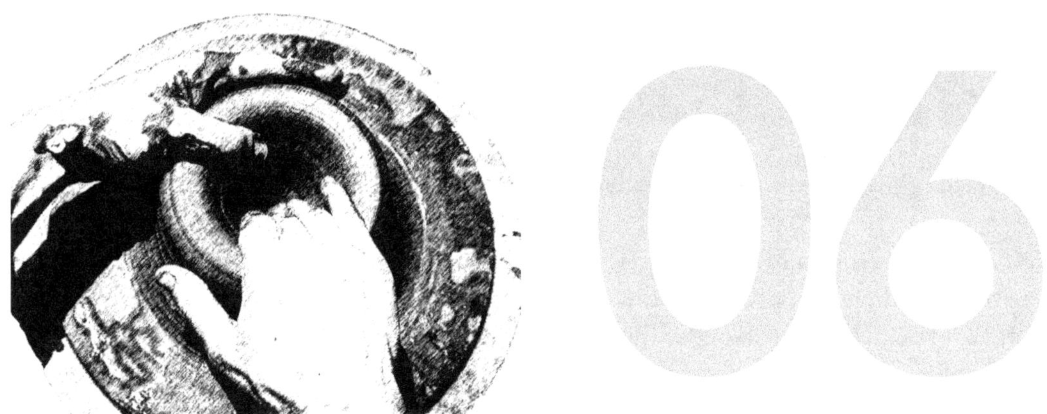

OPENING

The clay sits on the wheel, smooth, round, and perfectly centered. But there is a problem. The lump is solid through and through. There is no opening that will turn the heavy lump of clay into a bowl, a cup, or a vase. At this point in the process, there is too much in the way, and it is of no use at all. So the wheel spins and the potter gets to work, resting his left hand lightly on the outside of the clay, using his right hand to press into the top of the clay. He moves the extra clay aside; he opens up an empty space. As the clay is opened up, new room is made available to hold good things.

INTRODUCTION

Creating empty space requires trust. Work, e-mails, serving in ministry, reading, studying—keeping busy with activities like these can make us feel useful and accomplished. But by creating space of solitude, silence, and rest, we turn over our time to God, saying, "This is for you to use. I want to draw my purpose from you." When we create space for God to enter into our lives and use us, we reach our full potential.

Throughout this session, be sure to focus on opening as both an "emptying" and a "filling" process. Yes, we deliberately open up space for God. But there are also proactive steps, namely spiritual disciplines, we can take to ensure nothing else takes that place. If you are doing a Lenten study, this chapter particularly applies to the traditional practices of Lent.

DISCUSSION QUESTIONS

GIVING UP

"The problem is that we are not very useful when we are full of ourselves. God can fill us and use us only when we clear the way, leave some room, and cultivate an open, empty space."

What do you tend to fill your time with? From where do you draw your purpose? Spend some time thinking and praying about your weekly schedule. Can you identify any specific things that you need to push out of the way to make room for the whisper of God?

Sin can fill our lives, keeping us from being fully used by God, but so can other things that we would typically think of as "good," such as shopping, good food, music, relationships, a great book, even serving. These are not bad in themselves, but when do they become vices? What such things might be taking control of your life?

BEING FILLED

"Ultimately, each discipline serves the same purpose: creating an empty space into which God can pour those good things he has prepared for us from before the foundation of the world."

Take a closer look at the disciplines listed in the chapter: solitude, silence, fasting, and releasing. All four facilitate a listening mindset. Studying Scripture, reading devotionals, praying, and worshipping are all important actions, but so often we get caught up in our own voices and thoughts, missing the still, small voice of God. When was the last time you actively listened for God? How would our lives look different if we set aside space to listen, and fully expect him to speak?

KEY QUOTE

"Pray, worship, watch, listen. God can speak to us in many ways. In the book of Job, chapter 38 and 40, we read that God answered Job out of the whirlwind. And so he can. But more often, it seems that we must make room in our schedules, our homes, and our hearts so that we may hear his voice (Psalm 116:1), recognize his voice (Judges 18), listen carefully to his voice (Exodus 15:26), pay attention to his voice (Exodus 23:21), and obey his voice (Exodus 19:5)."

KEY SCRIPTURES

Have members of the group take turns looking up and reading these passages:

1 Kings 19:11-13
Psalm 37
Luke 10:38-42

NEXT STEPS

Consciously set aside time each day this week to open up space just between you and the Lord. Choose one or two of the disciplines mentioned—solitude, silence, fasting, releasing, or a combination—and intentionally pursue that each day. Journal your responses, and come back next week ready to share the results.

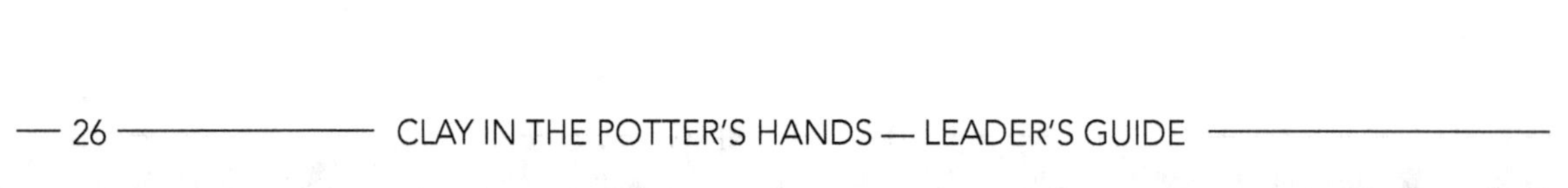

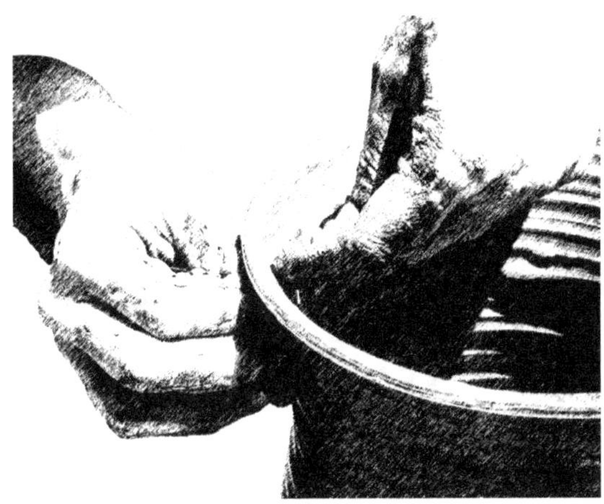

SHAPING

This is the moment of truth, the moment the potter has been waiting for. Every step before this one is preparation; every step after is finishing work. In shaping a pot, the potter puts one hand on the inside of the pot and one hand on the outside, squeezing the clay in-between, moving from the bottom to the top. The clay is stretched, thinned, and directed between the potter's hands. As each person is shaped according to God's plan, so each pot is shaped according to the potter's will. One day he makes coffee mugs and mixing bowls for the kitchen. Another day he crafts a slender vase for the living room. But whether he is creating a pot because there is a need for something to function in the household, a need for beauty somewhere in the world, or a need to express the joy of creativity, he makes each pot as he sees fit.

INTRODUCTION

In the pottery process, this is the moment of truth. And now our study shifts, from preparing for the life God has for us to stepping into the fullness of his promise, as he shapes and transforms us into true works of love and art.

During this week's session, focus on bringing troubles, especially concerns for the future, before God. Yes, we are commanded to follow him by faith no matter our circumstances. But he also invites us to wonder and ask honest, earnest questions.

DISCUSSION QUESTIONS

TAKING SHAPE

"Each pot is shaped according to the potter's will. One day I might make coffee mugs, cereal bowls, tea pots, or mixing bowls because I need something useful for my kitchen. Another day I might make a slender vase because I need something beautiful for my living room."

Think about the shape of your past. Is there an unexpected turn of events that didn't make sense at the time, but now is a clear indication of God's good and perfect will? Share that story with someone this week. It will be an encouragement to them and to you.

QUESTIONING GOD

"God answers honest questions and honors those who seek him by addressing their concerns."

Read the story of Ananias together (Acts 9). Have you ever experienced a similar situation? Have you ever been called by the Lord to go a certain direction, but it didn't seem to make sense?

Imagine Jesus is sitting in the room with you right now. What questions would you ask him about your life and his will for you? What concerns about the past, present, or future would you bring before him? Share your thoughts, and then pray together, presenting your worries before God.

SURRENDERING IN FAITH

"Either God is our Lord and we say yes to his will in his time in his way, or he is not Lord, and we say no to what he is calling us to do."

Think about the shape of your future. In your heart, are you clear about saying an unconditional "Yes!" to Jesus, the Lord? Together, ask for God's help to identify these areas of resistance and understand them and work through them.

KEY QUOTE

"He may explain things with great clarity and purpose. Or he may be stubbornly silent on the matter. In either case, at some point or another he will say, "Go!" And that's exactly what we must do."

KEY SCRIPTURES

Have members of the group take turns looking up and reading these passages:

Isaiah 45:9
Proverbs 3:5-8
Philippians 2:1-11

God shapes each of us uniquely, but at the same time, we are all being shaped after the example Jesus set. His perfect life of humility and submission to God's will is a shining light for us to follow as we submit to the hand of the Potter.

NEXT STEPS

Return to that last question concerning the shape of your future. What is standing in the way of you giving God an unconditional "Yes!"? This week, work on those specific areas of resistance—those areas in which you haven't relinquished control; those places that you haven't given over to God for shaping.

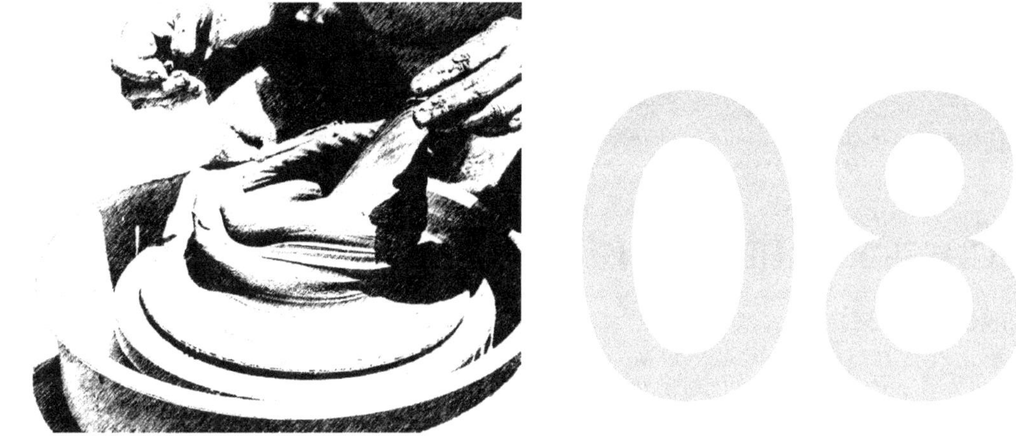

RESTORING

As the potter is working, something goes wrong. The clay was perfectly formed just a minute ago. But suddenly, it wobbles, warps, and tumbles over. What would cause a pot to collapse like that? Sometimes, if the clay has been pulled and stretched too much, water seeps in between the flat plates that make up the clay and weakens its structure. It's called "clay fatigue." And it may seem like a disaster. But the potter is never daunted. There is always something he can do. He scoops up the clay, takes it over to the wedging table, and begins again, pressing and turning, eliminating pockets of air, softening dry places, returning strength and integrity to the entire lump of clay. Then the potter attaches it to the wheel head, sets the wheel spinning, and simply starts the process all over again.

INTRODUCTION

Up to this point in our study, each step has gone smoothly. The potter has accomplished all of the initial steps. The pot is coming into shape. God has been working in our hearts, shaping us, molding us, guiding us. Our horizons look bright. We have great hope and feel closer to God than maybe ever before.

But what does the potter do when his clay weakens, wobbles, and collapses under the stress? Does he strip it off the wheel, throw it out, and begin with a new piece of clay? No, he perseveres. Just as our God does with us when we falter in our walk with him. When we grow tired under the stress of life and can't seem to find the energy to continue.

In this world, and in our pursuit of God, something can always go wrong no matter what part of the process we are in. During this session, focus on the hope we have in a God who doesn't give up on us. Romans 8:38-39 reads, "Neither death nor life, neither angels nor demons, neither the present nor the future, nor any powers, neither height nor depth, nor anything else in all creation, will be able to separate us from the love of God that is in Christ Jesus our Lord." Nothing—no circumstances, no mistakes—can separate us from him as he continues to mold us.

DISCUSSION QUESTIONS

FACING FATIGUE

"Too many pulls, too much time, too much moisture, and the water will weaken the clay so much that the pot will simply flop over. Clay fatigue. Ever felt like you've been pulled one time too many and simply flopped right over?"

Fatigue is a fact of life for most of us. Consider if there is a need in your life right now to make changes that will bring refreshment and prevent the destruction to mind and body that comes from accumulated fatigue. Then consider: Is someone you know facing serious challenges in the push and pull of life? Is there something you (or your small group) can do this week to reduce the stress and help carry the load?

Think of a time when you faced a major setback—when things did not go smoothly, when the process was interrupted with an unexpected collapse. Do you have a testimony of the way that God can move into a situation and redeem it?

Just as the potter's wheel spins around and around in the same motion, so we often find ourselves stuck in the same routine of waking up in the morning, going to work, making meals, paying bills, running errands, taking care of responsibilities. It's easy to grow weary and burnt out. What small changes can you make in your routine that might refresh your day? It can be as simple as praying during your work commute, setting aside 5 minutes for silence in the morning, or writing an encouraging note each day to a loved one.

ALLOWING RESTORATION

"When the pot comes tumbling down, it may seem like a disaster. But the potter is never daunted. There is always something he can do."

Have you ever gone through an experience like this? When something went wrong in your life and it seemed everything could come crashing down? But as the book says, "The potter is never daunted. There is always something he can do." How might you live and respond to negative circumstances differently with this perspective?

KEY SCRIPTURES

Have members of the group take turns looking up and reading these passages:

Isaiah 1:18
Isaiah 40:28-31
Romans 8:28-30

NEXT STEPS

This week's "Next Step" is all about prayer. Because what else can we do in those moments when everything seems to be heading towards disaster, when we feel like there is nothing we can do to fix the situation, when we realize how our own efforts ultimately fall short? Identify an area or situation in your life that seems beyond repair, and pray regularly for its redemption and restoration.

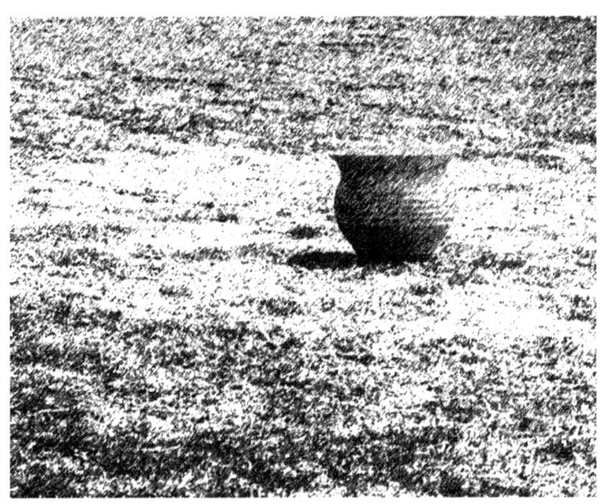

PERSISTING

Once the shaping process is complete, the potter removes the pot from the wheel. A thin piece of wire is held taut between the potter's fingers, and slid in-between the bottom of the pot and the surface of the wheel head. The pot is lifted from the wheel, put on a flat board, and set on a shelf to dry—cut loose, set aside, and left alone.

INTRODUCTION

In life, we are required to wait. A lot. We wait for our food at restaurants, we wait in lines at the grocery store. We wait for answers to e-mails, to phone calls, to texts. We lay awake at night waiting for sleep to come. We wait for answers to prayer. We wait expectantly for our Savior to return.

It seems waiting is an inherent part of life. And oftentimes, it causes feelings of loneliness and abandonment.

What is the key take-away from this chapter? God is still present. Even though you are waiting, even though he seems silent, he is with you and working in your life. Even when the clay pot is sitting on the shelf alone, the potter has not forgotten it.

DISCUSSION QUESTIONS

WAITING

"Waiting. Sitting. Silent. Untouched. Unnoticed. Until the work is thoroughly finished. This, too, is a necessary part of the process."

What are you waiting for right now? A response from a friend or family member? An opportunity at your work? An answer to a prayer? Or are you just waiting for the next step in your life to be revealed? Share your answers as a group.

CULTIVATING PATIENCE

"The pot has been set aside on purpose; this time of waiting is absolutely necessary."

Now, think about the situation you just shared. Are you waiting patiently for an answer? What makes it difficult for you to wait? How might you view the situation differently with the perspective that God is working in your life, even when you can't see it?

KEY QUOTE

"But God has not forgotten, and he is 'not slow in keeping his promise, as some understand slowness' 2 Peter 3:9. The example of the clay makes this clear. The potter has not forgotten the pot."

KEY SCRIPTURES

Have members of the group take turns looking up and reading these passages:

James 5:7-8
2 Peter 3:9

The Psalms are filled with poetic passages in which this psalmist describes the challenges and peace of waiting on the Lord. Pray through these Psalms together:

Psalm 27:13-14
Psalm 37:7
Psalm 130:5-6

NEXT STEPS

Take this week to practice patiently waiting. Consider mentally putting aside whatever you are anxiously waiting for, and press into the fact that it is resting in God's hands.

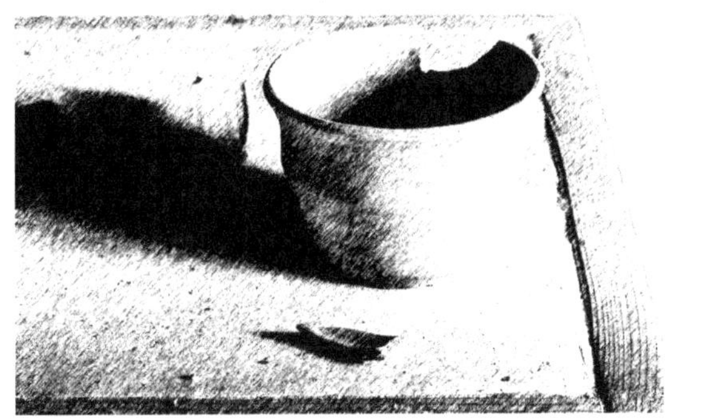  

RENEWING

During this dry time, the pot is extremely vulnerable: even gentle handling can cause chips, splits, and cracks. But a good potter can fix chips, smooth bumps, mend splits. And if the pot is seriously damaged, even shattered, the potter can renew the clay with water, reattach it to the wheel, and use the same clay to make a new pot—perhaps one even stronger and more beautiful than before.

INTRODUCTION

The pot is formed, the clay is dry. But it is far from finished, and at this stage in the process, it is still very fragile. The dry clay can easily crack, crumble, chip, split.

The author gets at the heart of this chapter here: "A good potter can take that very same clay and make that very same pot all over again. A very good potter can take that very same clay and make something even better."

During this session, set aside time to invite God's renewal. Worship God through song (see suggested songs in the back of this guide). Have a time of silence and listening for God's voice. Serve hot tea and coffee. In whatever ways work best for your group, make this meeting a refuge from the busyness and stress of everyday life—a quiet place open to the Spirit of God—so that group members leave renewed and refreshed.

DISCUSSION QUESTIONS

REMEMBER HIS FAITHFULNESS

"God can pick up the broken pieces of our lives, our ministries, our hearts, our hopes, our dreams. He can saturate them in the power of the Holy Spirit..."

Share stories of God's renewing power. Has there been a time in your life when everything around you seemed broken, yet God worked a miracle of healing? Has there been a time in your life when going through a season of hardship and brokenness resulted in a stronger you?

FIND HOPE IN HIS FAITHFULNESS

"New life for old, dry bones. It is one of the most powerful pictures in the Bible. It is one of the most beautiful promises of God. It is available for you."

Do you have broken pieces of some situation, some life dream, some relationship, some gift or ability that seem broken beyond repair? Share as a group, and rest in God's promise that nothing is beyond his renewing power.

MAKE AMENDS

Is there something that you have broken but have not yet made right—a promise, a commitment, perhaps a possession? Even when we are careful, our words and actions can be destructive, and we need to do everything in our power to make things right. Are there things that you need to do this week to make amends?

KEY QUOTE

"And God, the Master Potter, can make that very same pot all over again. Or maybe, just maybe, he will make something even better."

KEY SCRIPTURES

Have members of the group take turns looking up and reading these passages:

Ezekiel 37:1-14
Isaiah 35:5-7
2 Corinthians 4:16-18

NEXT STEPS

Do you have broken pieces of some situation, some life dream, some relationship, some gift or ability that seem broken beyond repair? Revisit your answers to this question, and decide on practical steps to take this week in trusting God to renew your life. Give your broken pieces to God in prayer—and see what he will do.

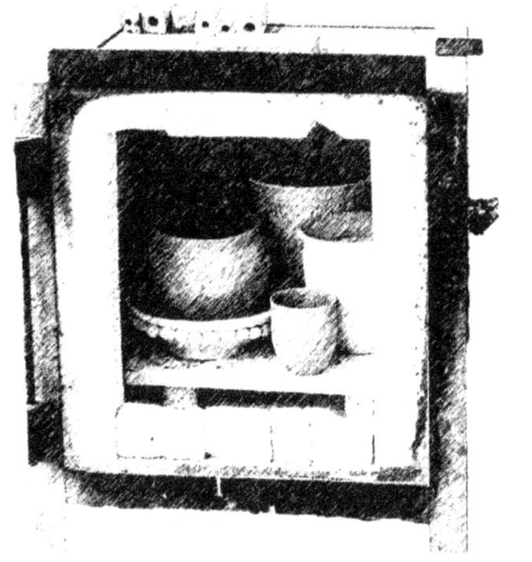

11

TRANSFORMING

The potter picks the greenware pot off the shelf and stacks it in the kiln. There have been many difficult times of cleaning, wedging, stretching, and drying. But now comes the very worst of it: the pot is flung into the blazing furnace. Hot. Very hot. Impossibly hot. The kiln heats the pot to about a thousand degrees Fahrenheit. The fire is scorching, and the fire is dangerous. But after it is fired, the pot is smaller, lighter, and much, much stronger. The firing process heats the clay so hot that a permanent change takes place; it will no longer dissolve in water. The process isn't easy or comfortable, but the clay pot is not good for anything until it is transformed by fire.

INTRODUCTION

Remember Chapter 9 on the challenge of waiting for the Lord? Well, waiting may have its challenges, but it also has its comforts. In those seasons of waiting, it's easy to kick back, relax, and live life according to our own rules.

But often, out of nowhere—like spreading wildfire—trials come. You get laid off at work. A friend breaks a promise. A family member gets sick. You can't make this month's rent. Your marriage is failing. You're losing hope.

"Consider it put joy, my brothers, whenever you face trials of many kinds" (James 1:2). Why? How is this possible? James continues with the answer: "because you know that the testing of your faith develops perseverance. Perseverance must finish its work so that you may be mature and complete, not lacking anything" (1:2-4).

Going through fire is not easy, enjoyable, or painless. But it is worth it.

DISCUSSION QUESTIONS

READY AND ALERT

"Waiting patiently is one thing. Waiting expectantly, alert and prepared, is even better."

Read and discuss the Parable of the Tenants (Mark 12:1-12), the Parable of the Ten Virgins (Matthew 25:1-13), and the Parable of the Talents (Matthew 25:14-30). Consider these questions:

— When life is going smoothly, it is easy to grow complacent, so that our faith is easily shaken when trials come. In our lives today, what does it mean to be alert and ready for the return of our master and prepared for whatever trials may come?
— In what ways does your life currently reflect this readiness? In what ways might you adjust your day to better reflect this awareness?

ENDURING THE FLAMES

The story of Shadrach, Meshach, and Abednego is central to this chapter. As followers of the true God, they literally enter the fire, endure the flames, and come out safely to great honor and praise from the king. Read the story together in Daniel 3:24-28 and discuss what this means in the context of our lives today, as followers of the very same God that was present in those defining moments so long ago.

IN THIS TOGETHER

"Pots are shaped alone, but they go through the fire together… In a similar way, God often gives us companions in the fiery trials of life, companions who can pray with us, talk with us, stand with us."

As a group going through this study, you can do exactly what the above quote says. Take time to allow each person to share any trials they are going through, and what they most need for others. Encouragement and affirmation? Accountability and conviction? Help with childcare, meals in time of sickness, or simply someone to regularly check up on them and see how they're doing? God has brought you together in this unique group, and you have the incredible chance to support one another through the flames life brings.

KEY QUOTE

"The fire is hot, and the fire is dangerous. It can bring about great harm. But although our enemies, and the Enemy of our Souls, may intend the fire for great harm, our God is able to use it to bring about great good."

KEY SCRIPTURES

Have members of the group take turns looking up and reading these passages:

Galatians 2:20
James 1:2-18
1 Thessalonians 5:16-18

NEXT STEPS

This week, we are seeking a change in perspective. It might sound crazy, it will be hard, but it will be worth it.

Consider the trials in your life—both the big ones and the small, everyday challenges you face. If it helps, make a list. This week, when you come up against these trials, thank God for them. Praise God that he has a plan for using these flames. And praise God that by leaning on him, you will come out stronger and better in the end. Transformed.

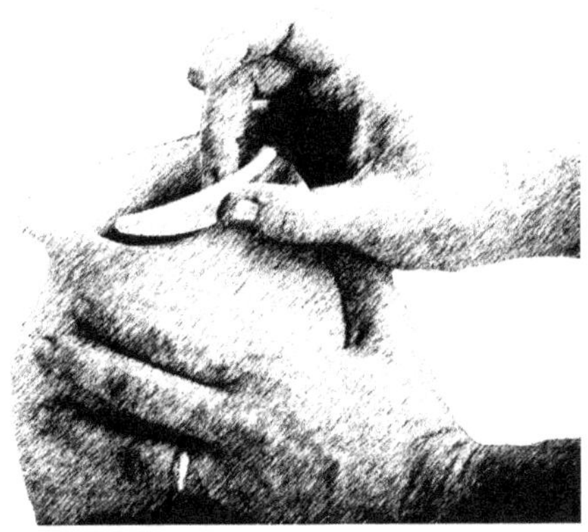

RENEWING

Now that it's been fired, the pot is very, very strong. But can anything be done if it gets broken? It has been permanently, unalterably, forever changed. Time has passed. And trials. It is rigid now. Strong. Hard. Water can't touch it. It won't dissolve. But a small chip, crack, or break can still be mended. It is not too late to redeem it. The potter gathers up the bits, dusts them off, reattaches them, and smooths them over. He uses a very strong bonding material—so strong, in fact, that the bonded place becomes stronger than the pot itself. If the pot is subjected to stress again, it will not break in the place that has been repaired. It becomes strongest in the broken places.

INTRODUCTION

In this chapter, we celebrate a beauty that is often overlooked, ignored, even avoided: the beauty of brokenness. The chapter says, *"It may be in brokenness that a pot achieves its highest purpose."* The stories of Gideon and the woman who anoints Jesus illustrate this truth. The story all of history hinges on—Christ's death and resurrection—illustrates this truth. And so can the individual stories of our own lives, played out day by day.

God is in the business of healing, and no chip, split, crack, or break is beyond his repair. In brokenness—in our weakness—his power and love shine brighter than ever. Begin your session for this chapter by thanking God for his power not only to create good, but to create good from the broken. To bring beauty from the ashes.

DISCUSSION QUESTIONS

TRUSTING THE LORD

Together, read the story of Gideon in Judges 7. Facing countless enemy soldiers, Gideon and his army of only 300 went to battle armed with trumpets, torches, and clay pots. This act of faith took incredible trust in God—a belief that he could use broken shards of clay to bring about a great victory for his people.

In the same way, we must trust God to use the brokenness of our lives to bring about victory. Are there worries, fears, needs, longing, injuries, or treasures locked tight inside your heart, things that need to be broken open and poured out at the feet of Jesus?

WILLING TO BE BROKEN

Read Mark 14:1-11. In this story, the woman breaks her alabaster jar of perfume to honor Jesus. As C. S. Lewis writes in *Letters to an American Lady*, "The precious alabaster box which one must break over the Holy Feet is one's heart." Christ not only requires trust in him, he requires a willingness to be broken—broken from temptation, broken from sin. Broken because, in humility, we realize we cannot make this journey on our own.

Together, consider what in your life God might be asking you to break away from. What might he be asking you to give up? In what areas are you depending solely on your own strength?

PRAYER FOR HEALING

Over the time of this study, hopefully your group has grown closer personally as you chase after understanding and following God more fully, and witness the same God shaping each of your unique lives. During this discussion, don't be afraid to dig deep. Focus on sharing areas, moments, and situations of brokenness in your lives. Where have you been broken? Where are you broken now?

Allow time for each person to share, and then pray for each specific situation. Depending on your group and size, you may want to have one person pray per person. However, it can often be most powerful to have a time of prayer set aside for each person right after they share their areas of brokenness, so all have a chance to lift him or her up.

This can be a very vulnerable process—but so is being broken.

KEY QUOTE

"The greatest moment in all of human history is a moment of brokenness. Christ willingly offered himself on the cross, a perfect sacrifice for the whole world.... God accomplished redemption that day. And the body of Christ, broken for you, was the means used by God to accomplish it."

Spend time in silence dwelling on this truth—that Christ was broken for you—and share any reflections or thoughts.

KEY SCRIPTURES

Have members of the group take turns looking up and reading these passages:

Matthew 5:1-12
1 Corinthians 1:20-31
2 Corinthians 12:9-10

NEXT STEPS

You prayed for each other during your meeting time—but prayer should not end there. Each person carries their brokenness with them day in and day out. Continue praying for one another this week, remembering that there is redemption, complete healing, and indescribable joy ahead.

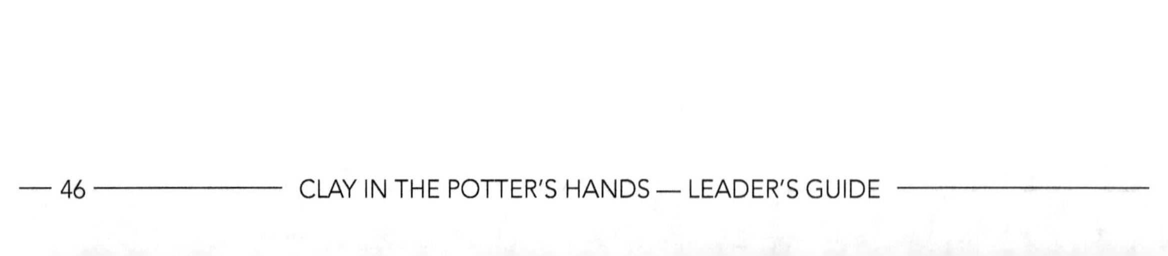

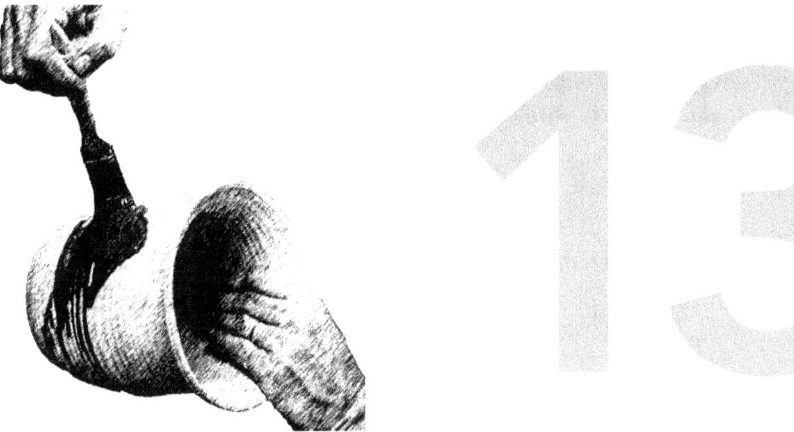

RETURNING

For the clay pot, the second time through the kiln is the step that brings out its full beauty. The potter brushes on a glaze, a thick suspension of chemicals that is basically tiny, tiny, tiny bits of glass. As the temperature rises, these bits melt and fuse together, covering the pot in bright color. The first time through the fire brings out the strength of the pot. The second time brings out its true beauty. It takes courage, lots of courage, to go back a second time, to return to a place of pain and challenge. But sometimes that is exactly what we are called to do. Go back. And do it again.

INTRODUCTION

We've been through the flames once, and that was hard, but we came out transformed. We've been chipped and cracked, but our Creator healed our brokenness.

But still, it's not smooth sailing from here. There is joy ahead, but also the pain of more fiery trials. And beyond that pain, a deep, deep strength and joy waiting for us if we will only trust and persist, even in the fire of the furnace. Even in the heat of the kiln.

DISCUSSION QUESTIONS

STORIES OF RETURNING

Stories have power. Especially true stories, about people who have endured situations similar to your own and triumphed. Take time to review and discuss each of the three Bible stories mentioned in this chapter: Joseph's brothers, Nehemiah, and Moses. How can these stories of faith guide you in your own challenges?

WE RETURN

"But to go through the fire a second time is another matter altogether. Sometimes that is exactly what we are called to do. Go back. And do it again."

Is there some task or situation that you have been afraid to face because you have been there before and it is too painful to imagine trying it again?

Is there some ongoing task that has become very nearly unbearable, but still you sense the need to stay and faithfully complete it? Together, ask God to transform the mundane into the miraculous so that you can see his hand even in the midst of this circumstance.

A PRAYER OF THANKS

"The second trip is infinitely harder than the first. But in the background is a whisper, and promise..."

Following Christ doesn't make life easy. Life is full of trials—and many seem to come at us again and again. Difficult relationships. Financial struggles. Lack of job security, health issues, or repeated temptations. But in the midst of this, we are called to give thanks. Have group members reflect on trials they have overcome in the past through God's provision, and thank God together that he has never and will never leave us.

KEY QUOTE

"The first time brings out the strength of the pot. The second time brings out its color and its true beauty. But it takes courage, lots of courage, to go back and go through it again."

KEY SCRIPTURES

Have members of the group take turns looking up and reading these passages:

Romans 5:2-5
1 Peter 1:3-9
1 Peter 4:12

NEXT STEPS

Go back to your answers for the "We Return" questions. Talk to God about them, and ask for the courage to persist in doing what is right. This week, focus on facing that pain and fear, knowing that God is working throughout the situation.

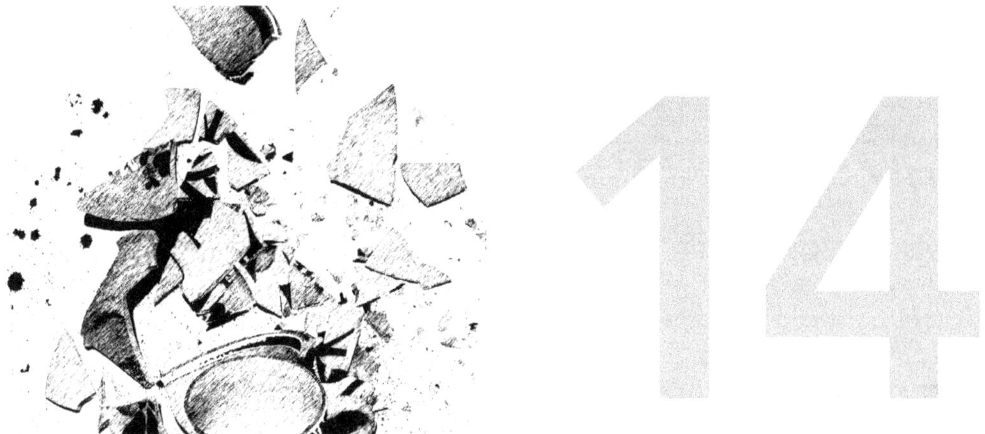

REDEEMING

There it sits, bright and beautiful, on the dining room table holding fresh flowers, or in the china cabinet waiting for a company meal. The pot is finished. But what would happen if this beautiful finished pot were dropped? Even at this point in the process, the potter can still move foreward. Undaunted, he prepares a clean, smooth surface and arranges the shards of the shattered pot in a pattern, gluing each piece into place and working grout in between the cracks. From broken shards he creates another thing of beauty—a mosaic. Broken tea cups, dinner plates, soup bowls, vases—all can take part in the miracle of redemption, joining old scraps together to create something of beauty and great worth. There is no raw material, no accident, no broken pieces that the potter can't redeem. Because no matter what, he is never, ever daunted.

INTRODUCTION

We have come far in our study. We are almost finished; we have answered hard questions and been challenged. The potter is almost finished; he has overcome many obstacles along the artistic process.

But what if the unthinkable happens—what if it all falls apart? What happens if the near-finished product shatters into hundreds of pieces?

Does the potter head for the broom and wastebasket? No. He perseveres. Just as our God does with us. Even when we completely blow it, fall over, crash and burn, he is never daunted. In this chapter, we come to terms with the fact that we are fallen human beings in need of a God who constantly restores and remakes us when we fail, and when we grow weary under the strain of life. The message of this chapter is not, therefore, a message of guilt, but of refreshing hope and restoration!

DISCUSSION QUESTIONS

NOTHING IS BEYOND HIM

"Even now, even at this point in the process, it is still possible for the potter to make things right."

Have group members each share moments or areas in which they tell themselves, "It's too late" or "This is beyond repair." Where have you given up hope? Where do you feel guilty or inadequate? Pray over one another, offering each specific instance to God.

A NEW CREATION

"The original ceramic piece served one purpose, and it was good in its season. The brand new ceramic piece will serve its purpose, too. And it is good in its season."

If possible, bring an art piece to your meeting that required the artist to redeem bits and pieces by making something brand new, such as a mosaic, a quilt, a collage, or a scrapbook.

To take this lesson a step further, take time to create such art pieces together. Supply, or ask group members to bring, such items as photographs, scraps of paper and fabric, chipped pottery and glue, pens and pencils, old magazine, and scissors. As you create, contemplate the truth that God takes the scraps and shards of our lives to create something beautiful.

KEY QUOTE

"Rightly understood, there is no raw material, no accident, no broken pieces, that our Creator God can't redeem. Because no matter what, God is never, ever, ever daunted."

KEY SCRIPTURES

Have members of the group take turns looking up and reading these passages:

Isaiah 44:22-23
John 10:7-10
Ephesians 1:3-10
Colossians 1:19-23

NEXT STEPS

Congratulations, you've almost made it through the whole study! It is suggested that you allow extra time for your last session, as you will all reflect back on the entire study. Ask your group to prepare for next week by reflecting on what they've learned so far and their hopes and desires for the future, after the study is done. It may be helpful for them to record this in their workbooks.

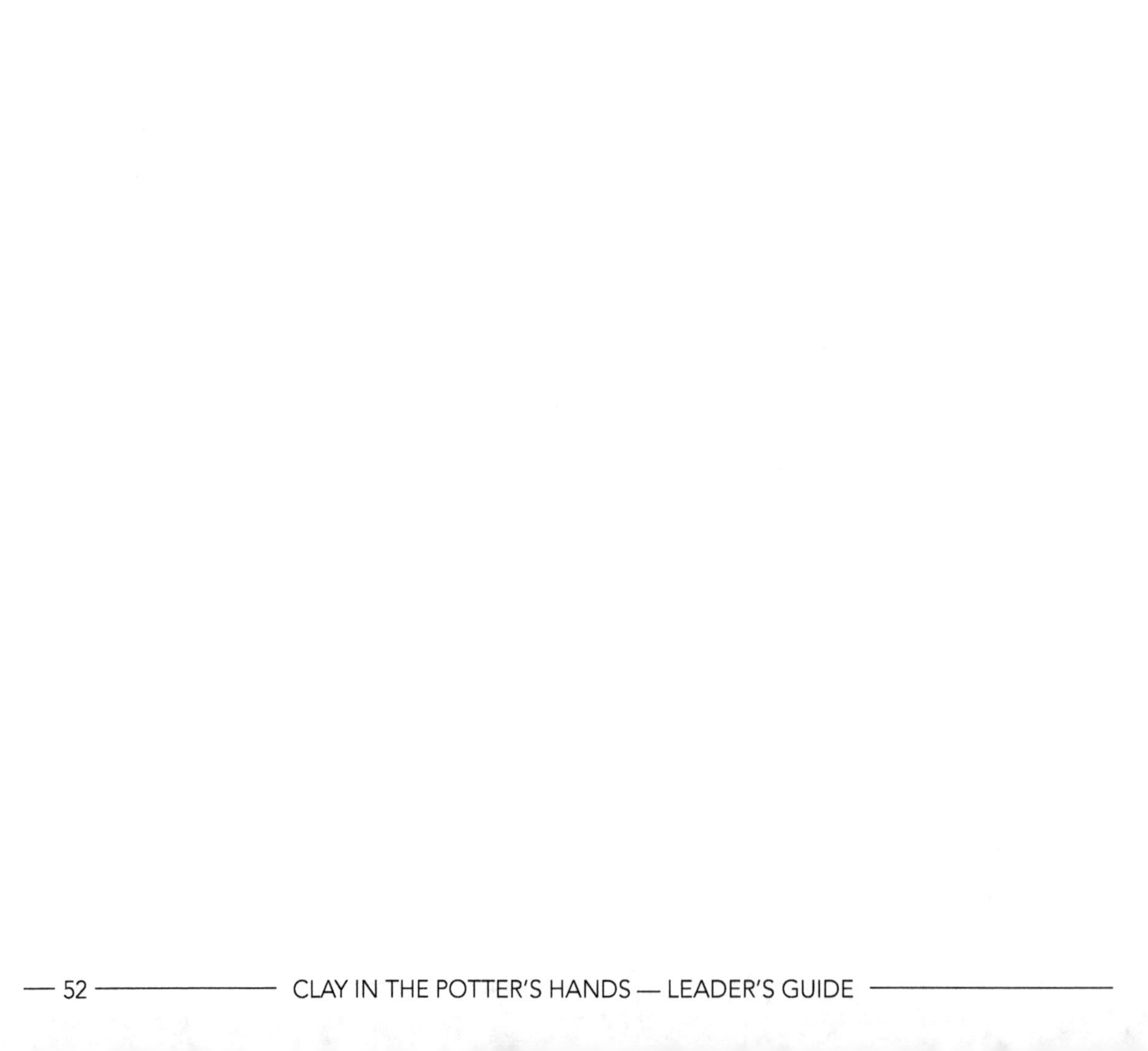

ABIDING

There it sits, bright and beautiful, on the dining room table holding fresh flowers, or in the china cabinet waiting for a company meal. The pot is finished. But what would happen if this beautiful finished pot were dropped? Even at this point in the process, the potter can still move foreward. Undaunted, he prepares a clean, smooth surface and arranges the shards of the shattered pot in a pattern, gluing each piece into place and working grout in between the cracks. From broken shards he creates another thing of beauty—a mosaic. Broken tea cups, dinner plates, soup bowls, vases—all can take part in the miracle of redemption, joining old scraps together to create something of beauty and great worth. There is no raw material, no accident, no broken pieces that the potter can't redeem. Because no matter what, he is never, ever daunted.

INTRODUCTION

We have reached the end. The pot has been shaped into the final project, forged through times of trials, hardship, and growth into something of great use, value, and beauty.

This marks the end of the pot's creation process, but it marks the beginning of a new life, holding flowers, hot soup, warm milk, cool water. And this marks the beginning of a new life for children of God: "If anyone is in Christ, the new creation has come: the old has gone, the new is here!" (Colossians 5:17). We are ready to be used by God, to play our part in his glorious plan, to serve and love others, and to simply abide in the presence of our Creator.

Share this truth with your group, and praise God together. But throughout this final session, also focus on the hope we have in the Lord when things do go wrong. The pot may be finished, but it can still encounter trials. Encourage your group by reminding them that no matter what chips, cracks, breaks, and falls we face ahead, God acts as our constant protector and redeemer, continually lovingly shaping and drawing back His children to him, no matter where we are in the process.

The steps we go through as God shapes us are not a list with steps we can check off, saying "Great, done with that one, let's move on!" Instead, we move forward and backwards and forwards again. In this life, we are constantly stretched and shaped. We go through many seasons facing the flames of the kiln, waiting on God, and healing from breaks and cracks.

DISCUSSION

LOOKING BACK

"The pot goes through the process once. Then it is finished. As we move through our lives, we find ourselves repeating various stages of the process.…. [God] needs to reshape and refine us afresh, until that great day when we are like Christ, when we see him face-to-face."

During this final session, take a look back at the past weeks and have some time for reflection and open sharing. Briefly review each of the chapters and ask the question, "What step in the process do you most relate to in this season of your life?" Chapter 15 features sentence summaries of each chapter that may help in this part of your discussion.

LOOKING AHEAD

"It has been a long journey from the stillness of the river bed…. We have seen how things look when all goes well. We have also seen that our sovereign God is not daunted by those events we think of as mistakes, missteps, sidetracks, and accidents. All these things work together for good!"

Finally, allow plenty of time for prayer at the end. You have come a long way together. Pray for each person's individual walk with the Lord, and then for your group as a whole. Thank God for what he has done and is doing in and through you. This study may have ended, but the journey ahead with the Potter has just begun.

KEY QUOTE

"Throughout our lives, God takes us back and forth through these steps, perfecting, refining, renewing, rebuilding. Unlike the human potter, the Divine Potter is never finished but always bringing about something new. In us. And through us. Now we have work to do."

KEY SCRIPTURES

Have members of the group take turns looking up and reading these passages:

John 15:1-17
Ephesians 4:22-24
1 Peter 1:3-9

NEXT STEPS

The "Next Step" will look differently for each person, depending on which step in the process they most identify with. Together, brainstorm specific ways you can use what you've learned in this study moving forward from the place you specifically are currently in.

Are there steps that you have been deliberately resisting, avoiding or neglecting? Ask God to make you willing to surrender even to that process.

SONGS FOR WORSHIP

GOD AS THE POTTER

"Have Thine Own Way, Lord" by Adelaid A. Pollard and George C. Stebbins

"Change My Heart, Oh God" by Eddie Espinosa

"The Potter's Hand" by Darlene Zschech

"Abba Father" by Carey Landry

SONGS FOR EACH CHAPTER

CHAPTER 1: CREATING

"The Stand" by Joel Houstons

CHAPTER 2: SEARCHING

"Amazing Grace" by John Newton

CHAPTER 3: PREPARING

"Hosanna" by Brooke Fraser

CHAPTER 4: COMMITTING

"I Have Decided to Follow Jesus" by Sadhu Sundar Singh and William Jensen Reynolds

CHAPTER 5: CENTERING

"Nearer My God to Thee" by Sarah Flower Adams

CHAPTER 6: OPENING

"The Heavenly Vision" ("Turn Your Eyes Upon Jesus") by Helen Howarth Lemmel

CHAPTER 7: SHAPING

"At the Foot of the Cross" by Kathryn Scott

CHAPTER 8: RESTORING

"Nearer, Still Nearer" by Leila N. Morris

CHAPTER 9: PERSISTING

"Be Still My Soul" by Katharina A. von Schlegel

CHAPTER 10: RENEWING
"Rock of Ages" by Augustus Montague Toplady

CHAPTER 11: TRANSFORMING
"Refiner's Fire" by Brian Doerksen

CHAPTER 12: REPAIRING
"Beautiful Things" by Gungor
"Great is Thy Faithfulness" by Thomas Chisholm and William M. Runyan

CHAPTER 13: RETURNING
"It Is Well With My Soul" by Horatio Spafford

CHAPTER 14: REDEEMING
"Jesus Paid It All" by Elvina M. Hall and John T. Grape

CHAPTER 15: ABIDING
"Abide With Me" by Henry Francis Lyte
"In the Garden" by C. Austin Miles

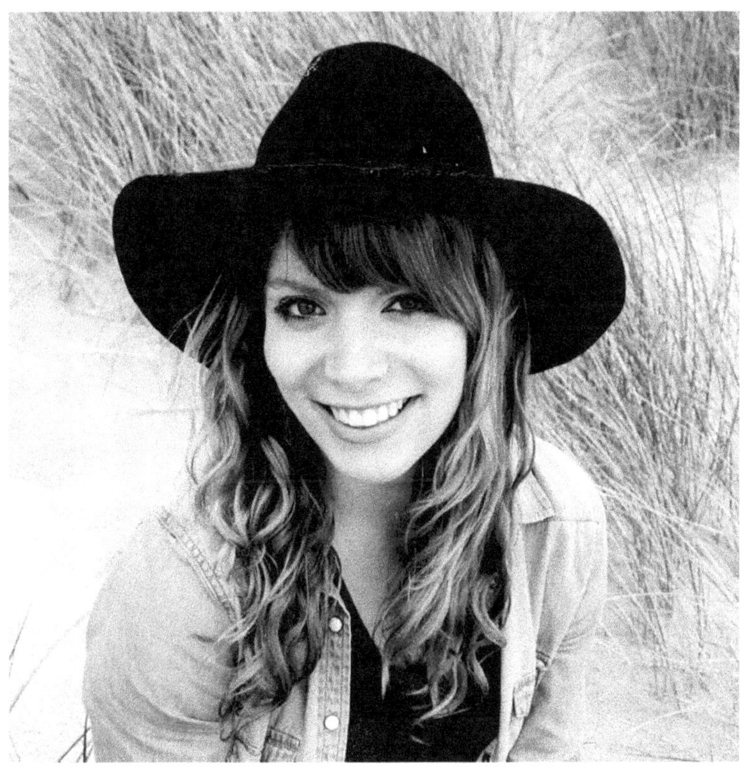

ABOUT BETHANY WAGNER

Bethany Wagner is a freelance writer and editor based in Seattle, where she also crafts stories and marketing pieces for Seattle Pacific University. She studied writing and theology at Azusa Pacific University.

FOR MORE INFORMATION, VISIT HER ONLINE AT

WWW.BETHANYCUMMINS.COM

NOTES

NOTES

NOTES

NOTES

NOTES

NOTES

NOTES

NOTES

NOTES

NOTES

NOTES

NOTES

NOTES

Clay in the Potter's Hands LEADER'S GUIDE: *Second Edition*
was designed and composed by
Matthew K. Tyler
in Arno Pro and Avenir
and published by

Lindale & Assoc.

A Division of TreeHouseStudios

www.ingramcontent.com/pod-product-compliance
Lightning Source LLC
LaVergne TN
LVHW080921110826
845155LV00039B/121

* 9 7 8 1 9 3 7 2 8 3 1 5 5 *